What's the Question?

by Ellen A. Goodenow

STECK-VAUGHN

Harcourt Supplemental Publishers

www.steck-vaughn.com

Here's a math game to play that's as fun as can be.
Name a question to go with each answer you see!

Answer: There are 10 of these in the air.
What's the question?

How many balloons are in the air?

Answer: There are 5 of these on this flower.
What's the question?

How many petals are on this flower?

Answer: There are 8 of these spinning away.

What's the question?

How many wheels are spinning away?

Answer: You can see only 1 of these in the night sky.

What's the question?

How many moons can you see in the night sky?

Answer: There are 8 of these in this pizza.

What's the question?

How many slices are in this pizza?

Answer: There are 4 of these on each square.

What's the question?

How many sides are on each square?

Answer: There are 13 of these on this flag.

What's the question?

How many stripes are on this flag?

Answer: There are 4 of these taking a look.

What's the question?

How many eyes are taking a look?

Answer: There are 6 of these on this door.

What's the question?

How many squares are on this door?

Answer: There are 7 of these on this vine.

What's the question?

How many green tomatoes are on this vine?

12

Answer: There are 4 of these perked up to listen.

What's the question?

How many ears are perked up to listen?

Answer: There are 12 of these on the ground.
What's the question?

How many feet are on the ground?

14

Answer: There are 4 of these in one dollar.

What's the question?

How many quarters are in one dollar?

Answer: There are 16 of these in this book.

What's the question?

How many pages are in this book?